FAT
JERSEY
BLUES

AKRON SERIES IN POETRY

FAT
JERSEY
BLUES

John Repp

The University of Akron Press
Akron, Ohio

18   17   16   15   14   5   4   3   2   1

ISBN: 978-1-937378-93-6 (cloth)
ISBN: 978-1-937378-94-3 (paper)
ISBN: 978-1-937378-95-0 (ePDF)
ISBN: 978-1-937378-96-7 (ePub)

LIBRARY OF CONGRESS CATALOGING-IN-PUBLICATION DATA

Repp, John.   Fat Jersey Blues / John Repp. — First edition.
pages cm. — (Akron Series In Poetry)
Includes bibliographical references.
ISBN 978-1-937378-93-6 (cloth : alk. paper) — ISBN 978-1-937378-94-3 (pbk. : alk. paper) — ISBN 978-1-937378-95-0 (epdf) — ISBN 978-1-937378-96-7 (epub)
I. Title.
PS3568.E68F38 2014
811'.54—dc23
2013039496

∞ The paper used in this publication meets the minimum requirements of ANSI/ NISO Z39.48–1992 (Permanence of Paper).

Cover: Photo courtesy John Repp
Cover design: Lauren McAndrews

Fat Jersey Blues was designed and typeset in Mrs. Eaves by Lauren McAndrews and printed on sixty-pound natural and bound by Bookmasters of Ashland, Ohio.

Kathy
(always)

back in the pines way back where the deer flies whine
back in the pines way back where the deer flies whine
my baby stomps stomps berries into wine

no more nothing where the cedar water glow
no more mama no more where the water glow
no moon where I run none where the black night go

got the fat Jersey blues got blues in my mouth
fat Jersey blues what put blood in my mouth
sing & dance all night never get gone from the south

—Junior J. Walter, "Fat Jersey Blues"

Contents

Trucking Flowers to the Dump
on a Day Like No Other

Big Vic drove. Little Vic rode shotgun, chewing the stub
of a dead stogie. The green pickup, hill of flowers

from that day's funerals. Ronnie & I squatted behind the cab,
shirtless kids in pith helmets. Best part of the job—floral wind,

drying sweat, afternoon shade of the cab, pre-dump stop at Scotty's
so Big Vic could tilt the ritual half-pint of vodka to the sky.

On the day like no other, we ferried two bums earning a day's pay,
Boss Bill a soft touch. They slowed down all we did & now sped up

the best part, every second free of the dead-still heat precious.
One bum pressed his forehead to his knees. My God, we all stank,

but they exceeded the reach of that word & all its synonyms.
Dressed in a filthy suit & tie, the other bum worked Q-tips

in & out his mouth, tossing bloody ones over the side as we rode.
Then the monumental stench of the dump, us raking a few minutes,

Q-Tip doing a good job with the push broom at the end.
Even then, I knew not to seek a lesson. Afternoon break,

I poured the last of my Hi-C into the red cup & drank it.

Reading *The Idiot* in Carleton House Apartments, Millville, New Jersey

Myshkin so serene at a ball or sipping tea
as someone labored to humiliate him. It took
weeks for him to board a carriage. Nothing
but noisy stillness, cascades of fevered,
microscopic speculations. The cover
was bordered in yellow, a Signet edition pulled
from the "Classics" shelf in the Cumberland Mall
Waldenbooks, or so I now propose. When at last

she arrived, Joni picked it up, said *Wow. Heavy.*
Later, we lay on the couch, just breathing.
The sleet that had splatted & ticked on the window
all day stopped. Frank next door pounded
down the stairs outside. Joni lifted her head,
smiled & nestled back down. It was enough right then.

Throwing a Ball South of the Pine Barrens

Throw a ball at the basement wall & catch it
one-handed on one bounce, white tennis ball too grey
with crumbs of mica & oil-furnace soot for higher play—
that was the game. A tipi (spelled "teepee") in the woods

hardly woods, but holy. The unforgettable watercress,
copperheads & far into fall, water rats. Dick saw Jane
& couldn't un-see her, not even pumping white gas
into the red, five-gallon can. Everyone said *geeus* & *wooder*.

"One never fails to kill fire fueled by the other,"
claimed the context clue. Dusty blue sky & biplanes
cutting their engines & revving up. When Jane dropped acid,
Dick cradled her permeable head & sang something far away,

where they didn't have to go, but could, so fragrant
& true he was, crumbling dry moss in his left hand.

Fact-Checking

Water moccasins, not copperheads. I fed her halvah,
not raspberries. The first time she'd eaten it, she said
as it crumbled going in. She was Jewish as my wife,
but I, addled joy, was first to feed her that sweet sand.

Hermit crabs, not blue & I never tipped oysters
down my throat. That was Bud, born 1920,
but the aromatic painter I should have kissed still wets
the tip of each new brush before swirling it in brilliant goo.

Her rapt silence failed to note my Verlaine-ish abjection,
even though I knew from Philadelphia. My mother's scoldings took,
so we never waded the creek in summer—too much poison,
no matter name & now poison is all the water is, dribbling under

the W.P.A. bridge where Mark gave me "Papa's Got a Brand-New Bag,"
not "My Girl," learning me for good, though I forget & forget.

Waiting for the Bus in the Reading Room of the Carnegie Library, Pittsburgh, Haggard in a Leather Armchair

I still had the Army-surplus field jacket & the beige-leather work gloves,
six of eight finger-seams shot, but rabbit-fur lining warm, oily, redolent
    of smoke.
I was happy as I ever got in those days to have missed the 61B that
    ferried me
to a private hell lower in the dank spiral than I can fathom now.
    I still had

the watch cap I bought at Kress & the hunting boots my father gave me,
the jeans & flannel shirt of my daily uniform & the dust motes left of a
    woman's love
& mine. What book did I carry in the jacket's big left pocket? Such
    consolation
to have one ready-to-hand in the cold. What satisfaction to have a
    corn muffin

in the right pocket & money enough for coffee & let's say Galway Kinnell
or *Daniel Deronda* or maybe even Proust to read. How dutiful to watch
    the clock
so as not to miss a chance to sink into the quiet chaos of that chopped-up
Point Breeze Victorian. Miss Frick lived five blocks away.
    The lawn bowlers

did their flanneled best on Sunday mornings. On each layover,
    the pilot fucked
a new woman overhead. They shrieked up there over the good coke &
    each other.

Why I Am Not a Performance Poet

I'm too morose too much of the time
or too cynical or not overt enough
in my politics—whatever they are this second
or this—or too satisfied with the material conditions
I've deluded myself into thinking I've earned
or too alert to narcissism (having spent decades
bent over the water) or too eager to defend
my own righteousness & my acute awareness of flaws
I've spent a lifetime basting with the hot fat
of flayed well-being or too old or not old enough
not to give a fuck & just get up there & bellow
or whisper or weep or too flummoxed by the need
to establish something called "cred" by stabbing
the air with one or two or all five digits,
torso tilted, one foot lifted a little off the floor
or too bored by the sledgehammer iambs & mock-opera spondees
or too much in love with books (a state impossible to imagine),
which performance poets nowadays seem to ignore
or disdain. I could be wrong. Maybe I've seen & heard
the wrong performance poets the twenty or thirty times
I've found myself baffled & assaulted thereby.
Carlos Robson did wet my eyes one night toward the end
of what he did. *Hey man, I'm only saying* as some would say.
I say "nowadays" because Ed Sanders & Tuli Kupferberg
not only performed poems so hilarious & profane & zapped
with zany joy it didn't matter they couldn't sing or play
the instruments they played, but also wrote & loved
& even sold books. Or The Last Poets, who deserve
their own poem or book of them. Or Gil Scott-Heron
before the drugs cooked him down to the Plato of cold cereal.
Or Patti Smith, at whom I yelled *Pitman! Glassboro! Mullica Hill!*
as she declaimed "Piss Factory" one night in Pittsburgh.
I envy performance poets, have tried & failed to become

a performance poet, yearn to clone the scop or troubadour
encoded in my genome, but my head's too big for hats,
let alone one of those cool straw porkpies performance poets
—male ones, usually—perch on the crowns of their heads.
Or those floppy things like the Dead-End Kids wore
or the vast, woolen sacks under which the dreads
I once yearned to grow will never pile tangled & sour,
poaching under stage lights at the Bitter End
or behind the Gates of Eden. Ah, well. Bless the heads
of poets performing. Bellow away. Whisper & weep.
That's what it comes down to.

Ode to Didi's Squash Stew & the Waitresses at Fred's Place

Paseo Pueblo del Sur, Taos, New Mexico

Just to eat & ogle at Fred's Place, I some days come this close
to barreling sleepless a day & a half to Taos, timing the trip
so I swoop in at 5:00 when I'll have the place as much to myself
as any Epicurean has a right to expect. O *piñon*-tang, O chile,

O winter solstice in the Rio Grande Gorge, I cannot fail to creak
through the door beyond which Red-Snake-Slithers-Across-Belly
leads me where Comes-Bobbling-in-Yellow will inscribe desire
& beam from on high. Unworthy supplicant from the bitter East,

I blurt, "Didi's, *por favor*" & she intones, "*Sopapillas?*" & I squeak, "*Si*"
with the certainty that honey & *agua* will appear unasked-for. As I wait,
cramps loosen, cartilage regenerates, carbuncles shrink, faith & hope
stumble from a putrid cellar & blink beneath celestial turquoise,

the high-desert naiads & looming food poultice to the ills
that hounded me here, the bourgeois bone-worrying that east
of the Continental Divide does not include beauty so toothsome
nor the bowl of zucchini, *salsa verde* & *frijoles* Nothing-Underneath

thrusts between my upturned palms. Before tucking in,
I contemplate her flexuous rear, the blue spider etched on her neck,
the Beelzebub Fred painted on the ceiling, the Madonna weeping,
a dozen doomed souls afire. Then I eat, existence a mouthful

of deep-fried dough, honey & stew, existence just
what the sages claim—ripe for devouring, poised to devour,
pollen, bee, sweetness & gone.

My Wife's Ass (or "You Annoy Me, Matthew Dickman!")

a reply to "Getting It Right"

"Your ass is a string quartet"? Which quadrant viola?
Which violin? What about the inevitable hairs?
Are they somehow the honey-yellow floorboards
of the metaphorical stage? Merely the gossamer
music's heat makes on the gut of bow & string?
"'Your ass is a shopping mall at Christmas'
wouldn't get Johnny Depp laid," my wife said
after I recited your ode to body parts as we lay
entwined on a Tuesday night in November.
"Your ass is Mick Taylor's third chorus
on 'Sympathy for the Devil,' Madison Square Garden,
right before Altamont," I said, relishing the smile
I knew I'd get because my wife gets all but a few
of my allusions & remains curious about the elusive ones
despite years of our warming the same bed.
I'm an Old Head, Matthew Dickman, but you can write—
high praise where I come from—yet please refrain
from ass-praise for at least a decade & practice decorum
about ankles, too, so purple in your telling they'd bear
not a flea's-worth of weight. Like you, I objectify
my woman & all her parts because she lets me, knowing
I'd do it regardless & despite this poem, my wife's ass
& our private contemplation of it have always been
classically proportioned & bare of metaphor.

Another Bourbon Poem

I wish I was a mole in the ground.
—Bascom Lamar Lunsford

It's raining & I haven't had a sip of bourbon in thirty years—
nothing go-to-meeting about it, just one too many nights
hearing Kevin bray *pussy farts!* till the Mecosta Oilers
lean their pool cues against the wall & click-scuff to his table
& he yells *dyke attack!* over & over as they escort him out
& everyone cheers & knocks whatever they have back.

I liked their uniforms—black with deep green lettering.
All of them were huge & fast. They hit home runs
before aluminum bats. Afterward, softball was pinball.
They beat the best men's fast-pitch team two years running.
We cleaned up. Kevin bought a generator for his camp.
Bourbon tastes like liquid mahogany. Carroll would bear

a tray of shots to the table & murmur our names as he set
each glass down. I tell everyone who'll listen how much
I love rain—right now, cold rain destined to become snow.
March & I already miss the dark. Thirty years is an eye-blink.
Carroll would say *That's a keeper* if you said something good.
I don't think of him often. If Kevin's alive, I'm Jesus Christ,

but how can those days & these & all the others I can't fit
into whatever I'm saying here be lived by one person?
Sometimes I'll sing a song in the car or my mind
& if I'm really singing, I'll not only know the answer
but know I've always known it, but then the song stops.
If you were here, I'd ask whether you know what I mean.

The Channel Deeper than Anyone Has Ever Known It, Except for the Implacable Scavenger

after Linda Lee Harper

When everyone reminds one of someone else
unthought till one sees bending for a dropped pack of gum
Jimmy from the painting crew or Bruno bearing a pocketful
of starry ganja soon to billow into the shady heat behind Unit 2
or Ingman wading through the playground scrum,
clicking his Beatle boots with the tacks in the heels,
or Drum resplendent in the canoe drifting down the Wading
or Joanne shoving the Moo Shoo Pork round the plate
while Lettie slugs Cuervo Gold & the fridge rattles so hard
the sugar cookies slide off & Jean trips trying to catch them
or Danny leaping into the Valley Avenue briars for the last baseball
or Melvin huffing a munchkin pile of coke off his knuckle
before lifting "You Are My Special Angel" into the ether
or Dottie picking her 'fro before tucking into the meat loaf
one of the three Daves calls Vegetarian Waterloo
or Karl frailing "Way Down the Old Plank Road"
with the fire roaring & the blizzard of whatever year that was
piling snow past the ridge pole or Billy slicing a backhand
& Judy whooping as the ball catches the line the way Billy's backhands
always do, scooting flat & dead toward the fence,
                                   one should say *Thank You*,
reread the Wisdom Books & Kierkegaard, take another run
at Meister Eckhart & at long last fall into Silence
& re-consecrate oneself to *what is* without the moony bliss
that phrase since the not-quite-post-Vietnam American seventies
calls up in those of us who first whiffed clove cigarettes
during the myriad blotto parties way back in the piney woods
we mistook for Arcadia.
            Ah. *Should*. Say grace

& one might do what one should till the time for *might*
has gone. New ones one sees seem old as one life
can hold. Doing doesn't go there, nor wanting,
nor even the gratitude at which *gratitude* merely nods.

Blueberry (or "Another Summer-of-1975 Poem")

The chains that bind us most closely
are the ones we have broken.
—Antonio Porchia

Gather with me in the kitchen where the floorboards
sag & squeak & Star's marbles veer
toward the northern corner unless
you put some serious oomph into your thumb.
Say *blueberry*. Say it sound by sound.
Cathy sits at the kitchen table with a friend.
Neither wears anything beneath her muslin blouse.
The helicopters have lifted off
the embassy roof. The house was built in the 1740s.
Dave & I have driven into the tidal flats
in his father's Willys. We ran out of gas near Bridgeton.
Read Kinnell's "Blackberry Eating" then my "Mulberry"
then finish this. Cathy & I will soon dunk in the Maurice River,
our cutoffs, my Pegasus t-shirt & her just-loose-enough blouse
tossed on the bank. Stand where I stand & you'll glimpse
the friend's puckered left nipple. You'll think, as I do,
If it does that when it's this hot, winter should be interesting.
For five minutes, say every word you think.
Notice what your mouth does. The floorboards are twelve
to fourteen inches wide. Some of the nail heads are big
as the smallest of Star's marbles. I no longer work
at the egg auction, but Nate does. He still talks about Auschwitz,
but only after his lunchtime schnapps. *Blueberry*. Mary spices
the pork roast on the drain board. The seedlings I've forced
for six weeks with liquid fertilizer & two fluorescents
in a closet lined with aluminum foil sit crammed
between the Willys' front seat & back gate.
The satellites that let us see the helicopters lift off
the embassy roof didn't exist ten years ago. *buhhhhllllloooooo.*
Cathy & the friend talk astrology. *What are you?*

Dave & I don't know, so they tell us they can tell
just by looking, which they do & we check & they're right.
We say *Wow*, elongating the *ow*. My mother's hair
has turned silver. Gemini hasn't been a space capsule
for eight years. Reading Kesey might help.
Richard Fariña. Alan Watts before he got famous.
Ram Dass, who goes without saying. Luckily, Dave's father
keeps a topped-off gas can behind the Willys' front seat.
My grandmother still roasts the world's best chicken.
George & Mike still work at the egg auction.
My mother has just turned fifty, which means inch-long hair,
swollen joints & a mania to make amends.
Mary beckons to Star, who skips in from the mud room.
Let's shuck this corn & they do. Dave & I listened
to *Paradise & Lunch* as we packed the seedlings
in the ice-cream-cone boxes a nymph named Maria
stacked for me outside the back door of Verona Custard.
buhhherrrrreeee. George only laughs when you ask
about Vietnam. Mike catalogs the dope, ordnance
& women (girls, really, as he always confides)
in descending order of power & enough detail
to fuel reverie & nightmare that seem like neither.
Mary's Dave comes out of the bathroom in a towel.
As soon as he's dressed, we'll head to the secret field.
Low-tide funk sweetens the kitchen. My grandmother still makes
the best peach pie in history. She worked twenty hours a day
between 1935 & 1941. Pine Barrens blueberries, the smaller the sweeter,
must be tasted to be believed. Go northwest of Hammonton,
past the cranberry bogs. My mother has never forgiven the Jews
who stiffed her at the Dells resort. They had the table manners
of five-year-olds. She smiled & smiled & got zero,
but then, nobody ever gave her anything. My father either.
My grandfathers, grandmothers, aunts & uncles either. Me?
I've been given everything & I mean that. Taste the peaches south
of the Black Horse Pike. Taste everything till no taste remains.
The seeds that became the forced seedlings Dave & Dave & I

will plant in the secret field rolled down the inner crease
of *Arthur (Or the Decline & Fall of the British Empire)*
into the ceramic bowl Joni bought at an old-timey music festival
in West Virginia & gave me because it was the right time
to give me that particular bowl, but also because I listened
so well & long into a hot night exactly one June ago to the tale
of the baby she gave up for adoption the spring
of her eighth-grade year. My grandmother still talks
about piecework on the Lower East Side, her friend Boyd, the El.
Notice what your mouth does with *peach*. With *Achilles*. With *sleep*.
At the veterans' home where I work, the World War I widows
have their own ward, the World War II widows theirs
& the Korean War widows three rooms with connecting doors.
Say *blueberry* sound by sound. Say each word beat by beat.
To help her escape some ugly history nobody talks about,
Mary & Dave let Cathy live up a hidden staircase
two inches wider than my shoulders. To walk the four steps
to the alcove under the eaves where she sleeps
on a twin-bed mattress over which she's nailed a shelf
that holds two candles, an incense burner & a paperback set
of *The Lord of the Rings* held upright by a pair
of marble-dove bookends, I have to hunch over a little.
I live in half a converted gas station with a tin shower stall,
paper curtains & a cat named Zar. Maybe some Neruda
would be good, certainly Bly wearing a dashiki
during his dulcimer period would be good.
My mother can't sleep. No matter what she does,
no sleep. I would dunk in the Maurice or any river with Joni
or her sister or the girl in purchasing with red hair
& body full of freckles who eats lunch with Nora,
the WAC from Morristown—but wait, Dave's ready,
so he & Dave & I wave goodbye, stride out to the yard,
lift the Willys' back gate, hoist two ice-cream-cone boxes each
& head across the corn field, down into a stand of cattails
& up a shallow slope into pine woods, then scrub oak & briars,
horseflies, Delaware Bay five miles west, gnats, sandy trail,

salt-punk-marsh-reek, no breeze, mosquitoes, white sky
through pine needles, sweat shining on both Daves' necks & arms,
sweat running down my sides, shoulders aching, forearms numb,
the seedlings rustling a little, serrated leaves deepest green,
dappled sun, bird cries, twigs & briars & pine cones scratching.
ssslllleeeeepuhhhh. My mother still listens to Paul Whiteman.
Joni introduced me to the word "clawhammer"
which I love almost as much as Dock Boggs clawhammering.
Helicopters *thwupthwupthwup* off all the world's embassy roofs.
Those left behind have bootstraps to fall back on & always did.
The secret field is long & wide as two of my tin shower stalls laid end-to-end.
My mother is dying & dying & dying, though nobody says a word about it.
On three sides, blueberry bushes eight feet high & I mean that,
secret blueberries Mary bakes in pies Dave & I have helped
disappear three times, blueberries sweet as those the Pineys sell,
big as the biggest of Star's marbles, the ball bearings
Dave brought home from Wheaton Glass.
The requisitions are blue at the veterans' home where I work.
Once a week, the attendants use garden hoses to rinse
the demented vets they've tied to wheelchairs with strips of sheet.
When Cathy showed me where she lived, she wore a chamois shirt,
beige, the top two buttons undone & Levis faded nearly white.
Sleet ticked on the window. The plane tree planted thirty years
before Bunker Hill clattered in the wind. I studied her collarbones,
the three creases at each temple. She said *We think the house-slave*
or maybe a couple or a family lived here. You believe that shit?
Kneel with me in the sandy loam, gnats thronging ears & eyes & nostrils.
Eat with me the secret fruit, salted by the sweat wetting our upper lips.
What a perfect spot for the noble weed, what a perfect long season,
what perfect, dusty, blue glories we shove in our mouths
once the planting's done. Forget meaning—for the second
or two it's possible, anyway. Wet or dry, bellies full or empty,
naked or spiffed-out in new pajamas, the demented vets
live where no one can find them. Taste the blueberry. Taste *blueberry*.

Notice what your mouth does. The helicopters glint way off. Mary slices the pork roast, spoons out the baked beans, reaches tongs into the pot for the white corn. In a few moments, the secret harvest & everything else will burn away.

Fat Freddy's Burnt Mill Blues

Freddy a fat man got no feet
Freddy a big man got no legs
got a good blue shirt
& a pair of wooden pegs

hot in Estelle Manor   hot in Marmora too
sweating down Egg Harbor   blazing up in the pines
Fat Freddy sing the blues
Old Nick make hot sixes nines

way long time ago Burnt Mill burn down
long   so long gone Burnt Mill burn down
nothing but cattails   all bitter & brown
dry mud underneath   all bitter & brown

pick notes fast all fly in the air
pick fast now float away in the breeze
never touch the ground   never stay nowhere
no-leg man won't ever freeze

Krishnamurti

Remarkable in July 1975 to find *Think on These Things*
on the "Religion" shelf in the Landis Avenue shop
now a pay-day loans storefront. *Autobiography of a Yogi*
& *Be Here Now*, too. In the post-industrial way of things,
Landis Avenue has vanished except for the street signs,
churches & Wainwright Funeral Home. I'm sorry to say
this is America, so the only bookstore in fifty miles
sells multicolored bibles, bad novels & trinkets
not just tacky but idolatrous. Paramahansa Yogananda
could fly. He talked with Jesus. In great excitement,
I told Kathy & Lois about his astral exploits
though each had taken Christ as her personal savior,
Lois by far the more pious, Kathy doing
our sociopathic boss on lunch break, saying *God knows*
my flesh is weak as she dabbed each ear with perfume.
Jesus had always awed & infuriated me, but no one knew.
He seemed everyone's excitement or quiet friend,
but a yogi who not only flew but chatted with God the Son?
How could you not marvel? We manipulated Royal
manual typewriters, none of us fast or cowed enough
for Walt, though I came closest. In the karmic way of things,
that vast plant has long since vanished, too, dust to dust,
pride goeth, lilies of the field. I found Krishnamurti dry.
Better the drenched *bhakti* adoration Ram Dass spread
like a Bosch banquet. Sitting in full lotus feels like flying,
but the severe Krishnamurti wore business suits.
He had Kafka eyes. Sitting in my red brocade armchair,
I'd read a few pages at a time & try not to think
in my ticky-tacky home on Cedarville Road.

Having Come Late to Kenneth Koch

Fifty-seven, I've come late to Kenneth Koch & the goofiness
of nouns & adjectives, the jig of Technicolor abstraction,
the mouthfuls of impossible food & happy longing,
but here I am reading Kenneth Koch,
who fought in the Battle of Leyte Gulf, about which I read
in my father's recliner before counting worms
& tying leaders, the striped bass off Barnegat Light
still running, many other vanished beauties, too.
I've written often of the heat, the salt, the way I'd ruminate
over battles & baseball games & you'd never know
for Nebraska-cornfield-sized swaths of Kenneth Koch
that he'd seen combat, which reminds me of Sam Esposito,
a hero of my life (& yours if you'd known him) who'd blow
on his coffee & whisper *Semper Fi* when all us hippie & National Guard
& peacetime-Marine knuckleheads screamed about the war.
It no longer matters where or when any of this happened
because it's mythic & true that Sam Esposito bulldozed corpses
on Iwo Jima, came home to Marie, spent decades bearing her
wherever she needed to go & heard us yell every day
about peace & war. Kenneth Koch would have liked Sam,
especially when he was most goofy, clambering up the thirty-foot firs
to string Christmas lights. Reading Kenneth Koch, I imagine poet & hero
scaring up Kurt Vonnegut for a long night's unwinding
over beer & roast beef sandwiches & sour pickles at The Oaks,
where they leave you alone till everything's empty
then fill it up again till you're good & ready to go.
As they shamble with snow in their hair down the boulevard,
Kurt shakes out a smoke & offers the pack & they all light up,
three men who know what's what, silent in the bitter cold.

Another Harvey-Pekar-Is-Dead Poem

I'll never now befriend Harvey Pekar, nor he me,
though I delight in imagining how he'd hate
"never now" & "nor," the snooty need to fiddle & falsify,
but I'd chuckle him out of it, the friendship we'll never have
sunk in the fecund muck of misanthropy, fed by the food
of winter, the two of us cocking ears toward the speakers,
reverence for the past, reverence for the bent note—O Harvey,
I can't help ornamenting our nonexistent bond!
Snow squalls have nearly killed me three times since I first heard you moan
about supermarket checkout lines & bus stops, General Electric & hippies,
pretense & pain. I huddled under my woeful blanket,
snow whistling sideways, furnace pilot blown out, coffee cold,
Wang Wei shut, you open—quality stock, Harvey, four-color cover,
splendiferous Cleveland winter, files shuttled down hallways,
clothes bins rooted-through on Saturdays, a buck for the drunk
snoring against a mailbox on Superior, the friend I should have been
right next to you at the party when you ignored the host's baby,
the audiophile gear filling one wall more precious than the saliva-slick blob—
my God, the kid'll grow & eat & talk, but we may never again gaze
at a $500 stylus nor go home quite so glad for the Philco Wireless
through which Bascom Lamar Lunsford wishes he was a mole in the ground
any time we want.

The Boy & the Bisbings

No matter what (& they endured plague after plague during silent,
     fogbound years
of what), the Bisbings sat each Sunday in the first pew, mild faces lifted
to the wrath of Donchez, who could turn "suffer the little children"
into a steppe of suffering at the almost-there end of which Vladivostok
lay reeking of soap cauldrons & dead dray horses under blue-black
     thunderheads
the year round. The silver hair of the Bisbings glinted in the candlelight—
her pin curls, his back-of-the-head fringe. No matter how hard he worked
to believe, the boy in the balcony loathed the smelling-of-mothballs Bisbings,
whose Bible-school lessons could turn the Four Horsemen of the Apocalypse
into warm milk, "Jesus loves us" their answer to every question,
Mrs. Bisbing's ankles crossed, Mr. Bisbing in his one brown suit,
hands upturned on his knees. How could they sit there
so silent & mild if the stories the boy heard over Sunday dinner
were true? God kept nailing the feet & hands of the Bisbings
& they kept swallowing the cubes of bread & drinking the grape juice
& saying "Bless you" with broken spears lodged in their livers as they bowed
to each one passing into the day once the Doxology had mercifully come.
How could Donchez buy the hot loaves at dawn, cut them, build a pyramid
of cubes in the silver tray & fill shot glasses with juice as the Sabbath brightened
then flay us between the Lord's Prayer & the hymns? Why did we
     return & return?
Under the sod the meat & meaning of the Bisbings. Under the sod Donchez.
Up in the choir loft the boy, all the organ stops pulled out.

Crystal Meth Under Her Choir Robe

No surprise. Bills to pay, pain to obliterate,
a favor to a friend desperate
for more time before facing facts,
or a reason less beholden to one-day-at-a-time
or I-don't-know-why or There-is-no-why-
I-just-like-getting-high or Then-Jesus-spoke-to-me
blather. Nothing's enough, not even the moments
when her voice—any voice, my voice—
vanishes into the Voice the hymn
wrenches from the throats of the spiritual
paupers up there swaying in black satin.
The God of the Garden is the God
of Chemistry, too, a single sniff
in a lifetime proof enough—nothing
can slough errands or heartbreak
so fast into the metaphysical ditch
where all of it belongs. Weren't we made
for better than the Fall, if Fall this is?
We all see what the Flood keeps doing.
A little while dry, please, a little while
with no chattering chimp between
the ears & the Wizard once more in Oz.
This is my mind, not hers. She's a story
I heard. I'm a story I can't stop hearing.
A plastic tarp in a monsoon may be
her future. A plush ride home to havoc.
A vision that delivers her from want,
deserving or not.

Nothing Happened

after C.K. Williams

Nothing happened in the dark stairwell
but what she allowed to happen. Our tongues did what tongues do.
Her mouth tasted of caramel corn. I forgot her name
long ago, but when this visits me,
I hunger for it. She wore a purple, ribbed top. My hand went
where it always tried to go
& she let it, languid in the mildewed stairwell
of the Traymore Hotel. When my friends & I said *Nothing happened*,
we meant *She wouldn't let me fuck her*. When this visits me,
I assure myself nothing happened though I already know it.
She let me do whatever I did. Some of us had never
done it or *done anything* (as we also said),
but good luck then or since
sussing out who had or hadn't.
I'd seen her on the boardwalk, leaning against the railing.
The wind tossed her hair, a wiry, shoulder-length tangle of black ringlets.
I walked up & said things & she laughed, a miracle during the moments
she laughed in the night wind off the surf & a miracle each time
I've recalled it. What was I doing in the Traymore Hotel?
Wherever I went, I went there for the rest of the night.
She wore thin gold hoops in her ears
& a braided leather thong around her left wrist.
Whatever happened next involved Sunday newspapers
on the beach with her family, the surf folding over itself,
morning breeze cool. Someone fiddled with a transistor radio
the whole time, the father glaring & silent as we all read.
She wore a blue bikini. *My God* is all I can say about what that meant.
After awhile, she grabbed my hand & tugged me past
the jumble of blankets & towels & coolers up the beach & across
    the boardwalk
into the lobby of the grand hotel gone sagging & mildewed & up
the stairs & into a chaotic room with a canopied bed.

My fear of the father had vanished the moment
she ran her free hand through the black ringlets
that haloed her head as we strolled nearly naked
across the boards in the sun. Though nothing happened,
I wish it had. She turned to me at the foot of the bed
& lifted her arms round my neck & rested her forehead
on my chest & poof—nothing. If she revealed more
than she already had, surely I'd remember. I can smell the salt
in her hair this second. I was seventeen in Atlantic City
& walked the threadbare carpet of the Traymore Hotel barefoot.

Sand Road Stomp (Slight Return)

cold   hungry   no moon up there
up there   up there   no moon up there

dance so you fly   dance so you fly
way over the pines   oh high over the pines

bury me here in the summertime
bury me here in the summertime

roast a pig all night drowned in wine
roast a pig & toast me sometime

Bob Johnson

Bob Johnson liked to yank his shirt up to show his scars.
"They took part of my kidney," he'd say, or "They fixed
my heart" or "They cut into my stomach." We were seventeen,
Bob Johnson's scars whiter than his translucent skin.
As if that weren't enough, he had knock-knees
& a harelip. We'd say, "How you go down on a girl
looking like that?" or "How's your tongue fit through there?"
We ragged one another without mercy, Johns Thoden & Ball
worst of all & they still had what they'd been born with.
Bob Johnson was fat & we told him that all the time.
His laugh had a whistle in it. He laughed a lot. "The truth hurts,"
the cliché says. "The truth will set you free," quoth St. John.
Bob Johnson in a coat & tie was a sight to behold.
He thrust his hands into his pockets & set his feet wide
like a car salesman. Like many of ours, his father worked
at Kimble Glass & was twice as fat as his son. We loved
Bob Johnson & he us. We saw the truth in one another
& give or take the tricks of hormones & memory told it.

What Happens to the Circus

Very well then I contradict myself.
—Walt Whitman

The one circus I've witnessed
exists only in a crumbling poem
that says things I'd never say now
& rue saying then, despite the wisdom
of letting go rue & the past,
which has never existed, but if it had,
elephants lumbering in a blue tent
would have killed it & if they'd failed,
the ghosts who bear my name as they melt
in the Fortescue sun with barbecue grease
shining on their fingers would have done
the job till it was dead done, as nobody says
anymore, but should. A book I just read called
the circus sad by nature. Fake & bitter the circus
said the book I enjoyed because it showed
how the circus in the form we know it
hearkens back to the Middle Ages,
an unimaginable time if one imagines it well,
a time without privacy or given names,
at least for the peasantry.
I mean the European Middle Ages,
of course. I love knowing
how people lived in the deep past,
or at least the best, most detailed & vivid guess
about what they ate & celebrated & how.
We originated there somehow, the ancestors
dust eventually, but not for a long time.
I originated on an aluminum bench
in Battery Park, enjoying the jugglers
& the aroma of roasted chestnuts. I was born
on a bus to Bridgeville, reading *Medieval People*

before typing & schmoozing for eight hours.
I was conceived & baptized on the mythic green couch,
Toby Tyler propped on my stomach.
The yellow dust jacket. The trains & wagons
from which he gaped at things rolling by.
The tent poles & cruelties & gratitude for food.
I oversimplify. I sop black bread in the trencher.
Come one, come all. The barn-sour horse
clops round & round the tiny track
on a nowhere Saturday evening that softens & softens.

Beatrice

My first Beatrice vanished around a corner
on a tandem bicycle in the snow. My second
did everything a nineteen-year-old male
hadn't yet known to want & now wears
an onyx mussel shell pendant & heals
in the name of Jesus. If a Beatrice
can have black hair, my third wore
a permanent pea coat. It was cold that spring.
Dante may eschew possessive pronouns in the vicinity
of Beatrice, but not me. Mine are all mine.
I hold a photograph of—which one are you?
Ah, the willowy one in Washington. Polka-dot shift
in a June breeze outside the tapas restaurant. Good wine.
Nibble these little things & breathe the aroma of Paradise.
I will, thank you. I want nothing from you but exaltation.
Avalon is everywhere & sometimes I not only believe that
but don't think about it. I'm forever flat on my back
on a creek bank outside Austerlitz, New York.
That Beatrice exacted a fearsome price paid
with a gladsome, flayed heart marinated for three days
in lemon juice, antifreeze & a pint of honey
Kabir himself slathered off the desert combs.
What a feast! Spain in August it wasn't, but I swear
I whiffed grilled anchovies in the humid murk
under the hemlock. Streak of white
in shoulder-length ringlets. Halvah crumbling
off fingers at midnight. When you've cruised
the avenues of Valhalla in a jacked-up Chevelle,
how could it be otherwise? Oh, hello! Which one are you?
Ah, the one with the brown pin-curls who asked,

"Would you like a *pizzelle*?" Oh my yes, but only
if you always pronounce it with that little lisp.
The mountain is so green this morning. I can imagine
the lupine. The blue butterflies. My beauties, I believe
I'll hike up & meet whomever I meet, or none.

Monotony (or "Another Chekhov Poem")

Ninety-five degrees & I imagine Chekhov
in a straw boater—superb posture, clear gaze,

hands resting atop a walking stick.
Chekhov bore it, no matter the "it,"

at least I want to think so, though it
doesn't help me bear the heat

or anything else. Long ago, E insisted
I read Chekhov during the hottest summer

in a lifetime of sultry insomnia
& with the mildness I'd employed

the other four thousand times she insisted
I read everything she had, I agreed.

Unkind? Perhaps, but you weren't
either one of us. Everyone loves

how Chekhov's refusal to judge
makes clear any judgment is yours

since things just exist in his tales,
just go on & on, everything clear

but motive. How much more realism
can anyone stand? That summer,

reading Chekhov, (E was right
to rave, of course), aware the city

housed millions of people living
just fine without Chekhov, I drove

to work early & idled, just past dusk,
under a plane tree, cool air blowing

out the vents, thermos of iced tea at hand,
the book open on my left knee. Everything

was clear. The job didn't go any better
if I got there early, but I kept doing it.

It was a redundant season. Chekhov agrees:
Breathing is monotony, silence fantasy—hum

of circulation, whine of nervous system.
It may never cool off, bear it or don't.

The Maltese Falcon

The Maltese Falcon premiered the year
Bob Dylan was born, the Japanese bombed Pearl Harbor
& my father worked the milk route with his brother,
which required sleeping through trigonometry.
It could've been the bread or egg route or even the tavern,
which hadn't yet burned down, but everyone worked,
that was the rule & I knew no one who didn't till one grandfather
left the sawmill at seventy-six & *aahed* into his wing chair
for two years to watch whatever the Philco Heinie & Al
bought him pulled in from Rhinelander. Three people remain
who know how he thumbed tobacco into his black pipe & slipped
his suspenders down before lighting up. All right, everyone didn't work,
sue me, at least kids under twelve in my generation didn't & how lucky
not to even have to think about hauling hot bricks to bed
or whether we'd survive what penicillin could now kill
or whether a raccoon would break into the outhouse,
which always seemed to happen past midnight in January.
Bob Dylan worked, too, sweeping his father's appliance store,
but how can you affix facts to someone who didn't become
Bob Dylan till no one knows when, maybe not even Bob Dylan?
At nine, my father formed hamburger patties by the thousand
& did forty or fifty other things now lost in Time's Sahara
before waking at three six days a week so Phil could rattle
the panel van around town, saying *Hurry up, Johnny* though my father ran
the milk or eggs or bread to the sleeping houses because Phil
only slowed down & *I'd be out of luck, but that was my brother Phil*
& what's high school next to that? This deserves a ballad
& a nameless genius to sing it. By 1942, Bud had gone to the war,
but not the Pacific, thank God, only England, but that was far enough
& meant more work for everyone else. My never-ending work
is to work to make this & everything else in our life's work true.
By the power vested in me as the writer of this poem,
I hereby treat all my blood kin to the Landis Theater premier

of *The Maltese Falcon*. In the damp heat October has failed to break,
they're decked out in seersucker & silk, delighted to shiver
in air-conditioning's miraculous chill. They fill the front row
of the balcony, the boys' feet propped on the rail, the girls' ankles
crossed on the floor. At the end, they stretch & yawn as Bogart
winces at the stuff dreams are made of.

Mayakovsky

Vladimir Mayakovsky was born a week after my grandmother.
Anna Wolf was nowhere near the poet Mayakovsky was,
but she didn't kill herself, either, the Depression her gulag,
the tavern's blazing kitchen her First Circle. Verbal tics
syncopated her tales, *I sez I sez* & *with that* & *up the city*
the Homeric epithets of my childhood. Technically, Mayakovsky
didn't suffer the gulag & my grandmother never went hungry,
but what they did suffer prepared them for more. She's dead
thirty years during which my offerings have gone uneaten
no matter the savor of crackling fat wafting toward the summit.
Life is no longer what it was, Vladimir, it's more so,

as it always is for the living. Depraved tattoos on ten-year-olds,
enameled cast-iron omelet pans, kidney transplants, Fentanyl,
vanishing planets, time itself not only arbitrary but slowing down.
What a woild said the crone in the aromatic motor home,
her phlegmy chuckle all that remained of vaudeville & the El.
You had to berl sheets in them days, so many sick, but no outhouses
in the city now, or anywhere else neither. I fed fire horses in Queens!
The sentence *Mayakovsky championed Futurism* baffles & uplifts,
a suicide-from-the-cradle nevertheless shearing doubt
off his wings long enough to make the next poem.
In 1915, Anna Wolf nursed two babies back from the brink,

rheumatic fever & typhoid at last passing away.
During a diphtheria siege, she coaxed me to drink
the elixir of whiskey, honey & lemon juice that till he died
reduced my father to tears of retrospective gratitude.
Poetry teaches what life does, that neither is enough.
The Russians can get away with sentences like that,
so I proclaim myself an honorary Futurist.

This line is a bowl holding a split peach & a fig
& this a cabbage simmering in chicken broth.
The Ancestors won't eat unless we climb back down,
so with that, I sez, what say we go up the city?

The Totossian Poem

The Totossians lived where we lived
before we moved across the Blackwater

because what had become their home
had settled so much in the two years

we lived there a marble set inside
the back door would roll

the length of the house & crack
off the molding under the phone table.

Dondero built three houses on sand fill
& we lived in two of them & bought

the third to rent, but that was years
& two windfalls later. My grandfather

was Austrian, so my mother knew
a little German, but three kids

& a hatred of cooking inspired
a walk across the W.P.A. bridge

to ask for lessons, Mrs. Totossian
having lived in Munich,

which my brother, being six
& in love with food called "munch,"

as in, "When's Mommy gonna go
munch again?" One night a week

she went munch & made yogurt,
Mrs. Totossian tending the crocks

between visits, my mother lugging
like a peasant two laden stew pots

across the creek, raw milk in quart jars
cramming half the fridge, warm yogurt

ladled into cereal bowls, then the spoon
of A&P jam & the German for "please"

& "thank you" & "I don't know,"
as in, "*Ich weiss nicht warum* Mr. Totossian

pulls weeds from the creek all summer
& never talks. *Ich weiss nicht warum* he looks

so red *oder warum* he plugs his mower
in the house *oder warum* I love walking

in the dark, *aber ich bin sehr froh*
when I do." *Sehr sehr froh* she was,

a thousand miles from home,
Vater tot, Kinder nothing *aber Kinder,*

Ich liebe dich the truth & a clearing
of the throat that meant something

hard would soon come.

Jumbo Pagano Might Have Work For You

said my father in two letters a year apart, but Jumbo Pagano
never came through, so I packed eggs & cut grass & lifted
things & set them down & drank Hawaiian Punch & stuffed
meatball subs down my throat & swallowed hot peppers whole
& spoke pidgin Puerto Rican & ogled the girls & huffed hash
& stripped my work shirt & rolled up my cuffs & sailed
my pith helmet through the white air behind Unit 2,
the ferocious sun cooking me
                                        & my father kept putting the word out,
saying *sorry for my grammar   maybe the union not Jumbo said no*
it'll work out   keep at it   my only sorrow a sorrow never to slacken—
the lack of a thousand letters in which he writes the why
& wherefore of his luminous & infuriating self in a hand
I'd know blind, a hand practiced in the vanished school
on Grove Road & perfected in the forty years of packing lists
& bills of sale & loan settlements & purchase agreements

that kept us dry in the deluge & cool in the heat & full of food.

The Bridge Over Blackwater Creek

I'm in the high desert again,
sage & juniper & creosote tang

suffusing air no breeze has troubled
all day. In the bright cold far

over the river, I open my mouth
to draw the acetic hush down deep,

where my father still slathers 4x4s
with a black, dripping brush as I watch

& want so much not to, want to walk
a coal-slick beam into the creek

with him watching as I ram it
into the post hole dug faster

than the current can fill it back in,
six black beams walked & rammed

with him gazing upon my *gravitas*
no matter pain, thirst, or heat raging,

work well done & wordless—but the job
has to get done & won't if he hands

me the brush to slop along the wood
or wraps his hand around mine to draw

the crosscut back along the penciled line.
I was a boy not strong enough yet

who climbed storybook mountains
in the damp, shrilling summers.

My father did everything that day
& ten thousand others. He cast

into the surf many midnights,
shoveled truckloads of fill

into the swamp & pinned bills
to the Ebner's Milk blotter

as the ancestral fires blazed. I love
the high desert beyond words.

I know a trail few others know
down the gorge, where today

ice will have grown into the current
though it's fast & deep. I mourn

my father's vanished strength,
the beard on the ancient face he cares

to clean no longer. He can do
nothing. Hiking in the winter

high desert makes a hunger I want
like no other, the acrid air

mine, all mine to breathe.

Final Food

For my father, lime Jell-O,
one quivering cube. He gags.

Water? No. Ice chip? No.
If I had the power, I'd spread

a quilt on a raft, blanket him
with roses, kiss his smooth head

—when did the skin get so taut
& supple there?—& push him

into the river as he begs
us to before they drain

two liters of fluid so he can
breathe longer. He says *Thanks.*

He lifts one hand. Peers at it.
Lets it fall. He has ice-blue eyes.

His beard has grown in blond.
All the magnificent hair

on the big black bear that growled
us to bed is gone. He sleeps

& wakes in gasps, ragged huffs
out his throat I hear, everything here

as he sleeps & wakes. He is
always here.

The Ocean City Poem

. . . go Rimbaud / go Johnny go . . .
—Patti Smith

Leaning on a lamppost after we buried our father,
I wear a fluttery smile. I could have bought the twitchy upturns
at each mouth corner if Woolworth still sold them. I don't feel
like a worm casing—I am the damp, aromatic, fecund thing itself
grown arms & hair & a belly pressing against a maroon shirt
& want nothing but to have been left behind the chill
nightcrawler undulating on & on through the lightless soil.
Jim's Lunch still sells crab cake sandwiches, still drapes a single leaf

of iceberg lettuce over the patty & serves tartar sauce on the side,
the little pleated cup chilled from its stay in the 1936 Frigidaire
behind the cash register with its steel crank & yellowed enamel grip
& walnut veneer I hunger to kiss. I say to the withered waitress
A thing is a joy forever & step into the air over High Street
for just a moment, gravity reciting its timeless tale once more,
but Jim's was Millville & this is Ocean City—not the Maryland obscenity

but the one that makes you buy your cherry vodka in Somers Point,
Marmora, or the whitewashed cube on the first corner inside Strathmere.
I is someone else & always has been, thank God, or this *This*
would vaporize the whitened, much thickened embodiment
of cliché & authentic feeling who wears a smile because Chris
wants a photograph & *wear* is what you do with a smile

after Father has strode into the church of cliché & wordlessness.
On a wall somewhere rests the photograph of the skiff
from which he first fished. Behind the wizened *I* laboring
to smile lies the ramp up which Ken, Chris & this body of mine
will walk to breathe the surf & say nothing & buy fudge

at the only shop on the boardwalk not closed for the season.
Fudge has always been too sweet for me, one of the few blessings

this mouth has always refused. I first breathed a girl's smoky hair
at the top of that ramp. She loosened her hold on my hand

& we fell together. Nothing does justice to the music pier
or the horseshoe crabs. Till the end of time, three men will drive
to Dividing Creek & on to Reed's Beach & come to rest

at the seawall in Fortescue. The bay will be calm, the tide out.
They will stand in the windy sun & breathe salt without hymn.

"The Ocean City Poem" has no use here. Nothing does.

Another Life-Goes-On Poem

My friend keeps a photograph
made just before her mother died

of their feet, bare on the ersatz
hardwood floor of the condo

the mother died in. *Try to tell
whose is whose.* Impossible.

All four broad with crooked toes,
balls nearly big as bunions,

tendons like the twine that bound
the grapefruit boxes my father

shipped by Railway Express
so his father could eat almost

fresh from the trees at the Miami
motor court he'd never see again.

I told how my grandmother
would push the oxygen mask

onto his forehead to spoon
the sugared sections in,

the tyrant holding sway
despite no wind for anything

but whispers, ankles like ripening
eggplants, callused palms

gone tender as his wife's cheek.
An Antarctica of pain between

my friend & her mother,
but something like peace

toward the end, or forgiveness,
though uttering such words

can presume too much,
even if you're one of the ones

drifting open water among the bergs.
With her brother, my friend shook

their mother's ashes into Tampa Bay.
Every Sunday for twenty-five years

my grandmother stood at the foot
of her husband's grave. We heard

how sick he was at the end,
how much he loved figs & citrus

& January in Florida after all
that work. She's lain next to him

for twenty-five years. Her body
let everything go at the end.

My friend & I compare feet
on the beach at Goat Rock,

gnarled toes wriggling
in cold wind, surf eating

our laughter. What a joke
to have walked this far

on those creatures down there.

Another Spanish Moss Poem

Though I've read shelves
of Civil War histories,
I know little of Georgia
but the Spanish moss my father
woke my mother to see
as we drove through Savannah.
She probably said, "Oh look, kids!"
& fluffed her hair. I'm sure
my father hung his arm down
the door & reminisced about riding
the train to Florida. My mother
filmed a few seconds of Birmingham,
the marvel of Christmas lights,
open windows & lush green.
We had two hundred dollars
& a steno pad for subtraction.
We hunted motels in balmy dark.
We had cousins to visit
& the marauding beggars
of Nuevo Laredo to fear
if we failed to squeeze
our pesos tight. During our picnic,
the last whooping cranes
tiptoed in the marsh. My mother
filmed the auction block
in San Antonio & the cantina
where we peered at the strange food.
All the cousins played football.
We saw Davy Crockett's broken knife
or Jim Bowie's. The battlefield
was buildings, but the musket balls
were real. We drove to Goliad
& saw my uncle off to work.

We slept between linen sheets.
The cousins ate cold enchiladas
& hot dogs slick from the package.
We left at dawn with a box of oranges.
In Georgia or Alabama, a trooper
stopped us & my father left with him.
My mother filmed the whole thing.
She said, "Oh, stop crying."
Nobody would go to jail.
We were just speeding, that's all.

Everywhere At Once

after Donna Masini

I can't be everywhere at once
my mother said, wrenching the wheel
as she zoomed me somewhere
in the black Chevy never to vroom
through another poem driven by a mother
who earned the peace no one will ever know
decades ago if suffering is payment,
which it is because I say so, invoice paid in full
as soon as this ends, oh dead, oh patient mother.

That same 1965 minute, 938,526,013 others
chorused their lack of omnipresence, children sullen
or starved, wailing or cowed, malarial or missing
a polo match because the Bentley threw a rod,
Africa still French this, Belgian that,
polio-fear dead ten years in our latitudes,
jets supersonic, Gemini a space capsule,
the moon & Mars, Orion & Calliope
mythic as in Homer or Keats, or nearly.

My mother was other, boy was she ever,
boy are we all, boy am I, jetting six miles
over eastern Indiana as Masini savages
her train-set-loving father, adores him,
hates every damp plank of the home
he kept afloat on the high seas
of Staten Island, bailing day & night,
in each fist a quart milk bottle
whose like I drained by the blue glass-full,

Ebner's Dairy mythic & mundane
as every childhood detail is & remains.
I don't need to read this book of hers,
don't need to stroke the nub
down to which each day wore a man
I can't know, no matter Masini's passion,
technique, willingness to forego sleep & love
& Lord knows to get down what can't be got,
but I do, because maybe she's got the last clue,

the astral lever, the golden mote—ah, Christ,
I don't need a book because I have it all by heart,
right down to the ludicrous hope for The Answer
I've just rehearsed for the last time, please,
please make it be the last time because everything
vanishes & I have to be the one to say *Enough*
so enough: My mother drove a black car
we all loved. My fierce mother got winched
into the ground thirty years ago. We hardly wept.

The thing on the bier rendered us mute.
The Chevy's twin exhausts spewed blue smoke.
When she'd had enough, she peeled out,
her three whelps rigid on the green couch,
Fireball XL-5 flickering on the Philco.
Three days before she died, she turned blue,
everything that meant something gone
for seventy-two hours, then thirty years.
We never asked where she'd gone when she sobbed

back in, ten years left to live, the *Fireball* marionettes
blinking lacquered eyelids, swiveling croquet-ball heads,
floating over the airless waste of some pretend planet,
resolution just over the etched horizon—

& the gossamer wires   & the dog chasing a biplane
& the cookies on a plate   & the milk in a blue glass
& my mother wailing her bottomless—what?
I don't know. I can't know. It's done. It's dust. It's all true.
We loved to bounce on the back seat of the black car.

The love in that house—

no more.

No Away

Grandfather retching in the parlor
where the hospice nurse hovers,
grandmother in a drugged sleep
in the back bedroom, frazzled mother
having said *Just go away*
the child wails *But there* is
no away!—that moment
myth now, decades on, myth
not mine, though when the tale

got told, I wept, vowing to bring
that shell to my ear whenever rage
& self-pity ebb, or when my son
asks why this dinosaur ate meat
& that one flew & why they're dead
& *What's a comet, Papa?*
Ice & rocks flying through space.
How's ice get up there?
It's very cold in space.

Is a comet coming now?
which tells me to change
the subject because I've just
finished reading about surgeons
manipulating microscopic scalpels
inside torsos a New Jersey
entrepreneur schlepped via
picnic cooler & van, then thawed
in his suite for two days so the flesh

would feel authentic. *You don't think*
about who they were because now
they're meat says a homicide cop
who sounds like a Zen master
toward whom I feel intermittent
devotion. Her *You are not*
this bag of skin has me staring
at the asymmetrical mole
inside my right elbow.

I love that elbow. I kiss
my son's elbow, his toes,
his Art Tatum fingers.
I kiss his mother everywhere
as often as possible
& you know where this
will end, don't you?
You can predict the very
words that will end this few

minutes with me, can't you?
Even though everything I write
reeks of what a category-loving
friend calls "late Romanticism,"
I am here to reflexively tell you
that I *am* here on an actual day
in Erie, Pennsylvania, sitting
at a black table in Barnes & Noble,
half-watching hundreds of cars

roar by, rare, early-spring sunlight
blaring through the mesh curtains,
a medical student pondering bone
pathology ten feet to my left, unaware
I'm fighting not to end this.
This is no fooling. I've got beloveds

I want immortal (in fact, I told
my shrink *immortality* this morning
when she asked what I most wanted),

though the wry tone I can't help
but use shouldn't fool you into thinking
I don't know the void my son's
outer-space book makes gorgeous
isn't. Inside this precious, irrelevant
pouch of flesh, I talk to you now,
right now, both of us every moment
at the end, where there *is* no away
& never has been, never.

Balcony

To wound the heart is to create it.
—Antonio Porchia

She lived at the end of the hall.
Once we'd driven the roommate out,

we lived at the end of hall
unless she'd exiled me

for some outrage trivial
as the oil on the Blimpie's subs

we gobbled on Fridays.
"Trivial" to the workaday drudge

I'd been raised to be. Oil glossy
on our mouths, burn of onion.

She exalted me. She'd have it
no other way. *Want* has never

been so weak a word.
We all but tore each other open.

We solved equations. We constructed
presentations & practiced

on one another. We played chess
& watched one another piss

into a Styrofoam cup.
We resumed reading or eating,

fucking or lying quiet inside
our breathing, our eternal—

my God, we were infants—
conjoined breath. On the balcony

in the cold dark, we let go
of the cup & watched spray

glitter on the hood of a car.
Once, far past midnight,

in the red bathrobe I loved
to untie, she swung a leg

over the rail & said *I'm done*
in a voice I'd never heard.

I begged, of course.
I said all the things

you'd expect. She came
back to me after awhile

& everything went back
to normal. I mean it.

You can stay young
for decades. It's easy.

There we are, lying
in a narrow bed, laughing.

The Mistake

I thought she was dead, but she's not.
Her letters will never die, not the one
in which she vivisects my cowardice
nor the one in which everything
is a lie nor the seventy-two other
crisping leaves I'll once more
bury where I can always find them.
Only touch remains inviolate
says Linda Lee Harper in a poem
hot from the digital ether
& right now I can't stand
any more wisdom than that
though *memory's worm* gleams
in the permanent moonlight pooled
on the porch where, cold & lonely
as a hundred country songs,
I touch a dying butt to a fresh one
& stare across the highway
as Scotty kills the beer lights
& she steps into the lot, her laugh
echoing in the still air. Sitting there,
I see myself sitting there
looking forlorn as I believe I am,
as usual so far inside the sorrow
I never want it to end. Claptrap
& love, undying love—same thing,
no-longer-dead strangers everywhere.

Another Mistake

Eyes green,
    not blue.

Red hair,
    no mistake there.

How could I
    not have known?

In the peeved
    paragraph after weather

(early snow there
    again that year)

& before "Love,"
    my permanent failure

to see & worse,
    my seeing of beauty

not hers in her.
    Therefore, it must

be a mistake—
    her: dead. Girl

in a white shift,
    eating the surprise

blueberries I biked
    to our permanent

picnic under the maple
    in front of Kerr Glass.

Down Teaburner Road

under the plane tree baby came to me
out of the green so green she ran to me
wet in the rain   wet in the rain

she said come inside get warm
come inside get warm, baby
so I drank down brandy in the coffee

fire in the wine & hot wind blowing through
fire in the wine all night in the hot wind
my baby & me wet in the black dark room

had a fine time in the room there
had a grand time rolling in the room there
where people in bad times hid & ran

through the rain in the dark a long way
through the rain in the dark a long way
where the sun peeked out maybe

under a plane tree in the sun maybe
under a plane tree in the sun maybe

Bats & Balls

The night I didn't stomp up the steps like a man—*her* man,
my hand clutching hers slick under the hot spruce in Giampietro Park
the day she confessed she'd given up the baby *swear swear*

you won't tell Greta—the back door looked far away as Burma
when Dan flipped Joe the fluorescent tennis ball, saying, "Me, I'd drag
the bitch out by her hair" as Old Testament mosquitoes burred

our haystack heads. Then the bats swooped & Joe broke out more balls
we flung into the all-but-liquid air, her in there with Viking Mark
of all people. Hadn't I strummed Neil Young's three chords,

nailed that falsetto California soul, gazed hard into the harsh daylight
of her motherhood? Her hair *would* braid a good rope. More & more bats
flapped from the chicken coop. Dead tennis balls littered the yard.

Dan really did say *Speaking of balls—where you keep yours?* If we'd known
who Socrates was, Dan would've been ours, but we'd grown up
in the swamp, where things were simple, ancient & imponderable.

Another "Taps" Poem

I played "Taps,"
the year uncertain, the war

Vietnam, the month May
or June, the graveyard Siloam.

I had broken through
to music on my horn.

Who died that I played?
Notes felt like milk

between my lips. "The war"
meant maps at school,

insignia on a mylar page
in a Golden Book

or encyclopedia, I can't
recall. I could go on

& have for too long,
but I want to know who

played "Taps" that warm day
thousands of miles free

of the war. I want to stand
where the bell of the horn

gives way to the air. I'm not
playing games, not with the balm

of mown grass in my nostrils.
Between my notes, the silence

of breeze & birdsong,
car noise & distant shouts.

I felt—I'm guessing—
proud to play in the silence

of whoever brought me where
the others stood silent above him.

Schoolhouse Door

In 1968, we held a vote
in American History.

I can feel the thrill
of being alone & righteous

in my passion for Wallace.
It often seems that soon

1968 will go from cliché
to forgotten, but I remember

pride when reading how Rizzo
kept the South Philly animals

caged. Soon, I soared way past
Young Americans for Freedom

& the Confederate battle flag
to a desiccated hinterland

on the von Mises frontier.
You could hunt what you needed

& pay in private currency.
I wore a "Socialism is Death"

button on my work shirt.
I had seen the beatings

on the news, the fire hoses
blasting girls in calico dresses

down the street, the hordes
plundering Newark & Detroit

& thought nothing too much
to teach what they had coming.

I miss how righting a wrong
would be the thrilling end of it,

how my own conversion tale
would soothe. *Mea culpas*

can crack the breastbone
& a .22 casing smell

like home. So few of us
have breathed the stench

of our labors.

Honorary Jew

The first year, I grated potatoes, chopped onions
& watched. The second year, I fed all but the eggs

into the machine & said *I'll do the latkes* & did,
my pile of crisp delights borne to the feast by the wife

who baffled me, our books closed, banter hushed,
money useless in the apartment—*house* my in-laws called it,

new-wave thump at one end, ganja reek at the other—
in which she'd knelt to tell the no one who listened

no more no   no more no   a three-year-old mouthing
the essential prayer. The uncle made rich by a song

stacked three & dug in, talking critics & Koch—
everyone crunching now, slathering applesauce, slurping tea—

talking Rabin & Mehitabel, radio & Durrell,
how a song is a poem or it isn't a song

& vice-versa. Done, he pointed a greasy finger
at me, said *You can't be a goy. You—I say it*

for all to hear—are an honorary Jew!
which, impossible dream, my latkes lived up to

for five more years. Then the wailing.
Then the dust.

Poem Beginning With a Line from Ezra Pound's "Canto XX" & Ending With a Line from "Notes for Canto CXX"

Turkey Point, New Jersey

You would be happy for the smell of that place
    at low tide, the heat outrunning metaphor
           & half the population of Gouldtown

contemplating the brackish run,
    crabs the size of dinner plates
           sidling into traps hauled up

glinting & dripping in long-unbreathed air,
    in shimmer of green through a horsefly wing,
           in shivering whispers the marsh grass whispers

this cold morning you choose to believe
    the brown stalks have things to say,
           the egret huddles down for warmth,

all is well under the graveyard sod in Fortescue.
    You with your roasted almonds & green apple!
           If it does—if now it does—

let the wind speak.

Canoeing the Lagoon

The morning heat
hasn't steamed in
& my muscles
haven't twitched their last,
so for now it's June,
cool mist twining
above the lilies,
two men casting
for largemouth they hope
are hungry, the channel
deeper than anyone
has ever known it.
I hand the paddle
from side to side,
gape at & fail to notice
the miracle of mundane
eye & elbow & thumb,
the gurgle the blade makes
when I plunge it in
& pull. It no longer
matters who taught me
what *stern* means.
I rented this thing
& soon must guide it back.

Hansey Creek Eel Blues

got me a bamboo pole & a chicken neck too
got a neck on a hook & I ain't no fool
black eel in the water'll feed me soon

fry it up   fry it up   baby   whiskey & fat
fry it up   fry it up   good whiskey & fat
all but the head   baby   like a shiny wet rat

oh when he died daddy said tie him to a board
daddy died sitting up said *tie me to a board*
float me down Hansey Creek to the mouth of the Lord

black eel in the creek said *wake up wake up*
black eel cut the creek said *wake up wake up*
stole my name that night   spit out a wooden cup

eel don't slither   eel don't fight
eel don't slither   he don't fight
swallow him down or you won't get right

Another Forgiveness Poem

May you from this moment ride
the elephant of acclaim as if born

to Brahmin elevation, born to the Elect,
Gloria in excelsis Deo, life without regret,

born to live out one fate unblurred,
a sentient hexagram conjured from yarrow

gathered on Mount Kinsman the June
the Big Snow of 1977 at last melted,

spring of vision & the road downward.
May you ride with no "as if" ahead,

the Apocalypse the thing seen staying seen.
May the water be sweet & cold,

may sleep be long, may work be glad
dancing for you, all of you swaying

up there in the sun, a column of quiet
riders from horizon to horizon,

tapping the great flanks with sticks
still damp with sap, reckoning me

& forgetting everything as you pass.

Notes

"Fat Jersey Blues": Junior J. Walter was a Pine Barrens bluesman so elusive some say he never lived. Collectors prize *The Minotola Tape* (also known as *Wheat Road Blues*), the single extant performance attributed to the singer. Captured in the Burnt Mill Tavern sometime in the early 1950s by an unknown fan using a wire recorder, "Fat Jersey Blues," "Sand Road Stomp," "Eel Blues," and "Teaburner Road" showcase Walter's sublime vocals and rhythmically ambitious guitar work. The collector Fuzzy Miner describes Walter's sound as "Satan in a good mood." Junior J. Walter's burial place has never been found.

"Ode to Didi's Squash Stew & the Waitresses at Fred's Place" is for Fred Muller.

"Blueberry (or 'Another Summer-of-1975-Poem')" is for Cathy Stassi, Dave and Mary Headrick, and for my old red-headed running buddy, David Graham.

"Another Harvey-Pekar-Is-Dead Poem" is for Karen Long.

"The Bridge Over Blackwater Creek," "Final Food," "Jumbo Pagano Might Have Work for You," and "The Ocean City Poem" remember John Walter Repp, Sr.

"Another Life-Goes-On Poem" is for Suzette Rochat.

"No Away" is for Katherine Knupp and Dylan Repp.

"Bats & Balls" is for Dan Kulp.

"Schoolhouse Door" is for Joe Freeman.

"Honorary Jew" remembers the songwriter and librettist Joe Darion.

I sing "Down Teaburner Road," "Fat Freddy's Burnt Mill Blues," "Hansey Creek Eel Blues," and "Sand Road Stomp (Slight Return)" for Joni Broeren, Bob Johnson, Donna Mendini, Andrew G. "Animal" Miner, F.R. (and his Harmony), Henry Robinson, William "Billy" Ruff, and Mike Starks.

Acknowledgments

Thanks to the editors of publications in which the following poems first appeared, sometimes in earlier versions:

Amethyst Arsenic: "Another 'Taps' Poem"

Blue Lake Review: "Another Harvey-Pekar-Is-Dead Poem"

The Cincinnati Review: "Jumbo Pagano Might Have Work for You"

Crazyhorse: "Poem Beginning With a Line from Ezra Pound's 'Canto XX' & Ending With a Line from 'Notes for Canto CXX'"

The Journal: "The Boy & the Bisbings," "Nothing Happened," and "Ode to Didi's Squash Stew & the Waitresses at Fred's Place"

Pinyon: "Another Life-Goes-On Poem"

Poetry: "Crystal Meth Under Her Choir Robe" and "Honorary Jew"

Poetrybay: "Blueberry (Or 'Another Summer-of-1975 Poem')"

The Portland Review: "Trucking Flowers to the Dump on a Day Like No Other"

Rhino: "No Away"

Slant: "Everywhere at Once"

South Jersey Underground: "Balcony"

Weave Magazine: "Another Spanish Moss Poem"

"No Away" was reprinted in *No Away* (Pudding House, 2007), winner of the 2006 "Give 'em Shelter" Chapbook Contest.

"Canoeing the Lagoon" and "Crystal Meth Under Her Choir Robe" were reprinted in *Music Over the Water*, a chapbook published by Alice Greene & Co. (2013).

Special thanks to Beth Zewe for the solace of the Spring House.

I owe a debt of gratitude to Linda Lee Harper for initiating a correspondence-in-poetry that yielded early versions of "Poem Beginning With a Line from Ezra Pound's 'Canto XX' & Ending With a Line from 'Notes for Canto CXX'," "The Channel Deeper than Anyone Has Ever Known It, Except for the Implacable Scavenger," "The Mistake," and "Another Forgiveness Poem."

John Repp is a widely published poet, fiction writer, essayist, and book critic. Since 1978, he has taught writing and literature at various colleges, universities, schools, and social service agencies. A native of southern New Jersey, he has lived for many years in northwestern Pennsylvania with his wife, the visual artist Katherine Knupp, and their son, Dylan.